Parent's Workbook

Parenting Your 1- to 4- Year-Old

by Michael H. Popkin, Ph.D.

Contributing Authors
Betsy Gard, Ph.D.
Marilyn Montgomery, Ph.D.

Photography by Stan Kaady

ISBN-10: 1-880283-17-4
ISBN-13: 978-1-880283-17-2

For my wife, Melody, a terrific parent.

Table of Contents

CHAPTER 1: **You and Your Child**

CHAPTER 2: **Preventing Problems**

CHAPTER 2: continued

CHAPTER 3: **Encouraging Positive Behavior**

You and Your Child

Parents Have a Special Job

If you are a parent, you have an important job. Your job is to protect your child. You also have a job to teach your child. Your child cannot survive or learn by himself. He needs **your** help.

Your job is to:

- keep him safe from danger

- give him healthy food, clothing, and a safe place to live

- help him stay healthy; take him to the doctor for check-ups and shots

- teach him to do things for himself

- love and nurture him

- teach him how to behave in useful ways

You are the most important person in the world to your child.

How will your child grow up? Will he help others? Will he hurt others? Your job as a parent is special. You can help him be a responsible person who can take care of himself and others when he grows up. You are the best person for this job.

The ideas in this book will help you. Remember, **you** are the parent. You will decide how to guide your child. Listen to your heart and your mind. We hope you will also use the ideas in this book.

As you think about parenting, do not worry about your mistakes. All parents make mistakes. The best thing you can do is learn from them. Do not blame yourself when you make a mistake. Think about what you can do better the next time. This will make you a better parent for your child.

Children Are Special People

We all know that children are different from adults because:

- They are smaller

- They do not know as much as adults

- They cannot talk like adults

Children are also different because:

- They think differently

- They do not always know what is dangerous

- They need to play (it is how they learn)

- They need adults to help them grow up well

Children are the same as adults in one important way:

- They have the same feelings: happy, sad, angry, and many other feelings

Your child will change a lot in the first 4 years of her life. These changes happen in stages. If you understand these stages, you will understand your child better. This program will explain the changes during each year: age 1, age 2, age 3, and age 4. This is why we call this program *1, 2, 3, 4 Parents!* Here are 4 names to describe each year and each stage:

Age 1 - The "Explorer"

Age 2 - The "Boss"

Age 3 - The "Pal"

Age 4 - The "Adventurer"

Children are different at each stage, and at each stage they learn something new. In fact, they cannot move on to the next stage until they learn certain things. Your job is to help your child learn these things and grow. You want her to learn to grow without hurting herself, other people, or things.

Age 1 - The "Explorer"

Your 1-year-old is just starting to learn about the world in this stage. He is seeing, hearing, touching, tasting, and smelling everything. This is how he learns. Exploring things will help him develop his mind and learn how things work.

Your child is learning to walk. He runs everywhere. He touches everything and tastes everything. This is great for his mind. But it can be dangerous. Your job is to make sure he learns about the world in a safe way.

While your 1-year-old is exploring, you need to protect him from danger.

Here are some ways you can make your child's world safe:

- Put away things that can break and things that may fall on top of her. Get down on the floor and see your house as your child sees it. What can she reach? What can hurt her? There are more of these tips in the "Making Your Home Safe Chart" on page 22.

- Make a safe place where your 1-year-old can play. You cannot play with your child every minute, so she needs to have a place to move and play by herself. Find a place where she can play without getting hurt or breaking something. Put up a safety gate to keep her in this safe place. There are more of these tips in the "Playing Safe Chart" on page 24.

- Always buckle your child in a safety seat while in the car. It is the law in all 50 states. Be a good role-model and wear a seatbelt, too.

- Never leave your child alone. This is not safe. If you are at home but cannot see or hear your child, check on her a lot. Be sure she is safe. If you take a nap, she should be in a safe crib or playpen.

- Make sure the toys your child plays with are made for 1-year-olds. Your child likes to put things in her mouth. So make sure that what she plays with is too big to go in her mouth and choke her. There is a list of safe toys for your 1-year-old in the "Playing to Learn Chart" on page 28.

- All children are curious. They want to know about everything. So give your child things she can learn with. Bring home a big cardboard box that she can climb in (make sure there are no staples). One-year-olds also love to play with plastic cups and lids. They love pots and pans, plastic tubs, and picture books. These things can keep them busy and happy for a long time. There are more of these ideas on page 28.

- You can begin to make rules for your child at this stage. But do not expect her to be able to follow them all the time. Sometimes she will forget that she should not throw toys. She may forget that she should not stand on a rocking chair. A child at age 1 forgets quickly. She is still learning to remember things. Stay calm and remind your child of how to act safely. You may need to take her away from dangerous places.

- Your child may try acting in a hurtful way. She may even try biting or kicking. When this happens, do not get angry or yell. Instead, look her in the eye. Say "No biting!" or "No kicking!" in a firm voice. If you get angry or start yelling, she may do it again to see if you will get mad again. We will learn more about discipline in Chapters 2 and 3.

Age 2 - The "Boss"

Your 2-year-old is learning about her abilities. She is learning how to get things done and how to make things happen. But she is also learning that she cannot always have things her way. Your child needs to learn to use her power in useful ways.

She will learn by testing you. She may do things she knows are wrong to make you angry. She wants to see if you mean what you say. That's why it is your job to say "no" sometimes. You will need to make the rules.

A 2-year-old is always testing her limits. Be sure to provide rules.

When you make rules for your 2-year-old, she will learn that "no" is a powerful word. Then she will try to use it on you! You need to stay calm. Your child must learn that "no" can be powerful. It has power when she uses it the right way. Later she will use this word when she says "no" to drugs. She will use "no" when she wants to stay away from danger.

Your 2-year-old will not know that following rules is how she learns. All she will know is that she wants her way. When you tell her "no," she will show her anger by crying and yelling. We will talk about this problem in Chapter 3.

Here are some things to remember:

- "No!" means a lot of things when a 2-year-old child says it. It can mean: "I do not feel good," or "I need a nap," or "Let me play more," or "I need some attention." Listen and look at your child. See why he is saying "no."

- Your 2-year-old still needs to explore, just like when he was 1. So you need to make your home safe for your child. But you also need to watch your child when you are outside. He should not walk away by himself. Be extra careful where there are lots of people, such as on city streets. Your child may run off when you are not looking. It only takes a second for an accident to happen.

- Your 2-year-old likes to play with other children, but he does not understand sharing. Two children will want the same toy. This may cause small fights. Try to distract your child with another toy. Also try to have 1 toy for each child.

- You may potty train your child at this age. Try to train him when he can stay dry for 2 to 3 hours. He should also be able to pull his pants up and down by himself. Girls are usually ready before boys. Boys sometimes need to be a little older. You may need to wait until your child is 2 1/2- to 3-years-old. That's OK. If you are worried, talk with a doctor or other professional about how to potty train. **Note**: Do not force your child or punish him when you are potty training. Instead, teach and encourage him.

Age 3 - The "Pal"

Three-year-olds love to play make-believe. And they enjoy playing with others.

At this stage your child will learn to play with others. She will learn what it means to have a friend. She will also learn about sharing and taking turns. The things she learns now will help her when she grows older.

Your 3-year-old knows some of the rules now. She is learning more about herself and doing more for herself. But she will get angry when she cannot do some things other children can do. She may see a friend riding a bigger tricycle. Or she may see someone using scissors. If she cannot do these things, she may get angry. That is normal.

Your 3-year-old has a great imagination. She may like to dress up in adult clothes. She will enjoy talking on her toy telephone and taking care of her baby dolls. She may even dress up like a man. She just wants to see what it feels like. She may also tell stories about herself that are not true. This is not lying. She is trying to learn the difference between the truth and "make-believe." She does not know that difference yet.

Here are some things to remember:

- Your child needs to play with other children. That will help her learn to share and be nice to her friends.

- Your 3-year-old still needs to have rules. For example, what happens if she does not take a nap? She still needs a nap, but she may not want one. She may fight with you. If she is too tired, she will not be fun to be around. She may fall asleep late in the afternoon and not sleep through the night. Make sure you still set rules so this does not happen.

- Watch to see when she is getting hungry, tired, or bored. These feelings can affect her mood. Feed her, give her a nap, or give her something to do **before** she gets cranky. When you think ahead, you will stop problems before they happen.

- Read books with her. She can look at the pictures and make up a story. This helps her learn. It is also a good time for you to be close to your child.

- Your 3-year-old will get angry because she cannot do some things. Help her find the things she can do. There are more ideas on page 28.

Age 4 - The "Adventurer"

Your 4-year-old is now ready to take risks. He is ready to learn what are safe risks and not-so-safe risks.

He is also learning to take care of himself. He wants to see how fast he can go and how loud he can yell. He wants to see what he can do by himself.

Your 4-year-old is ready to seek more adventure.

Your 4-year-old wants to know about everything. His mind is growing fast. He will ask "Why?" "Why?" "Why?" many times a day. Your answers will teach him about the world. He is also ready for pre-school. This is a great place for him to learn more about the world.

Your child moves faster now. He moves faster than he thinks. He may ride his bicycle into the street, or he may run in front of a car. He still needs to hold your hand sometimes. You need to be sure he is safe. You should still have rules he must obey.

Here are some things to remember:

- Let him help you do things. Encourage him for all the things he does, even if he makes a mistake. Let him do more things himself. For example, say, "You tried really hard" or "Now that you tried pouring your own milk, why don't you try putting the cap back on the milk carton?"

- Tell him what he **can** do before you tell him what he cannot do. For example, say, "You can ride in the driveway, but not in the street" instead of "Don't ride in the street!" He needs to know what is OK for him to do.

- Your 4-year-old still needs love and attention. You can hug him when you watch TV together and play. Let him sit in your lap when you read him a book.

- Keep him busy with interesting things to do. He may want to color a picture or play a game. Give him many kinds of things he can use when he plays. There are more ideas on page 28.

- Give him choices. For example, ask, "Do you want milk or juice to drink?" or "Do you want to wear your red sweater or your blue jacket?" This will help him learn to make good choices.

Ages and Stages Chart

Age 1	Age 2
The "Explorer"	The "Boss"

Age 1 — The "Explorer"

- Walks without help
- Sits in a chair by himself
- Says first words
- Knows different parts of the body
- Helps to put things away
- Likes to pull things out of drawers
- Uses hands and mouth to learn
- Loves to pull toys
- May try to bite people
- Is not ready to play well with other children
- Darts and dashes quickly
- May like to climb things

Age 2 — The "Boss"

- Likes to run
- Opens doors using the doorknob
- Touches her body
- Does not like to go to bed
- Does not like to share
- Likes to look at books and listen to you read
- Likes to undress and run around without wearing clothes
- Uses the word "no" a lot
- Wants to do things by herself
- Gets angry and yells
- Knows when she needs to go to the bathroom, but may lose control
- May begin potty training

⭐ Remember that all children are different. Some grow faster than others, and some grow slower than others. If your child is slower or faster than the chart, do not get upset. Be patient. If you have any questions, ask your child's doctor or nurse.

Age 3	Age 4
The "Pal"	The "Adventurer"

Age 3 — The "Pal"	Age 4 — The "Adventurer"
• Can ride a tricycle or bigwheel	• Can begin to copy big letters
• Can sing a song	• Asks all kinds of questions
• Asks a lot of questions like "What is that?" or "Where are you going?"	• Tells stories but sometimes gets confused about what is true and what is not true
• Asks "Why?" a lot	• Likes words and making sounds, such as rhymes
• Sometimes shares toys and takes turns	• Can tell you where he lives
• Can unzip large zippers	• Can use a knife to cut some foods
• Can talk about what she did yesterday	• Can zip his coat
• Likes to act silly	• Draws a picture that looks like something he knows
• Will play by herself	• May have bad dreams at night
• Wants to play with other children	• Girls want to learn about boys; boys want to learn about girls
• Will get angry if she cannot do things other people do	
• May be using the toilet, but may wear a diaper at night	

Children behave better when you use the "just right" parenting style.

Parenting Styles

As children go through these stages, parents try to teach them in different ways. In fact, we all have our own ways of doing things. The different ways we teach our children are called "styles." Some styles are not helpful. Often a style is "too hard" or "too soft" on children. Other styles are helpful. One helpful style is called the "just-right" style. Let's talk about these styles.

The "Too Hard" Style

Some parents want to control everything. They have a lot of rules. These parents use the "too hard" style. They do not let their children make many choices, and they punish their children a lot. They do not give their children many hugs, kisses, or encouragement. Our grandparents may have used this style, but it does not work well today. Today, parents who use the "too hard" style have children who become angry. They do things just to make their parents angry, too. When they become teenagers they will rebel.

For example, Latisha is 2-years-old. Her mother was watching a movie on TV. She told Latisha not to go near the TV. But Latisha saw the bright lights and went over to the TV. She pushed a button that changed the movie.

Her mother yelled, "I told you to stay away from that TV, Latisha!" Then her mother slapped Latisha's hand. Latisha cried.

Her mother said, "Stop crying! I cannot hear my show!" Then Latisha cried more.

Her mother said, "If you do not stop crying, I will give you something to cry about!" So Latisha left the room with her head down. She cried softly to herself.

Latisha's mother used the "too hard" style. She thought Latisha should follow a rule when Latisha is too young to follow it. Then she got too angry when Latisha could not follow this rule.

The "Too Soft" Style

Parents who use the "too soft" style let their children run wild. They have no rules. These parents may be too busy to teach their children, or they may not know how. They do not discipline their children. In fact, they spoil their children when they give them too many toys. Other times they may do things for their children that their children could do for themselves. These children may get "out of control."

WARNING: You cannot give your child too much love, such as hugs and encouragement. Love will never spoil your child. But you can give her too much freedom.

For example, Raoul is 4-years-old. One day he went to the grocery store with his father. Raoul ran around the store.

His father said softly, "Better not run, Raoul." But Raoul did not listen to him. Then Raoul's father did not watch Raoul. Raoul ran into some boxes, and they fell over. He kept running.

His father said, "Raoul, please stop." Then his father picked up the boxes.

Raoul said, "I want some ice cream."

"It is almost time for dinner," said his father.

"I don't care!" yelled Raoul. "I want some ice cream."

"OK," said his father. "If you will be quiet, I will get you some."

Raoul's father was being "too soft" when he let his son run wild in the store. He was "too soft" again when he let Raoul eat ice cream before dinner. Raoul's father did not set any rules.

The "Just-Right" Style

Parents who use this style are not "too hard" or "too soft." They understand that their children need rules. They know that sometimes children make mistakes. This is part of learning. They give their children lots of love and encouragement. They let their children make some choices. Parents will make mistakes, too. When they make a mistake, they learn. The next time they will act differently.

Mom remains firm and calm when disciplining her sons.

For example, Mother hugs Latisha and says to her, "I am sorry I yelled and slapped you when you touched the TV. I know you like the buttons. You are more important to me than the movie. Let's find something you can do. You can sit next to me and play while I finish watching the movie."

Raoul's dad can use the "just-right" style too. He can say, "When we are in the store, we do not run. You can walk with me or ride in the shopping cart instead. You are a big boy now. You can help me put things in the cart. When we get the shopping done, maybe we can buy some ice cream for dessert after dinner."

Most parents do not use just one style. Sometimes we are a little "too hard" and sometimes we are a little "too soft." Sometimes we are "just right." We will be better parents if we try to use the "just-right" style more and more. It is OK if we make mistakes. We learn from our mistakes. Our children learn when they make mistakes, too.

Keeping Your Child Safe

An important part of parenting "just right" is protecting your child. Young children want to learn and know everything. They do not understand that the world can be dangerous. Your home can be dangerous to a young child, too. For example, your child may want to know what is in the hole in the toilet. She wants to play with the

Young children do not know what is dangerous. You need to protect them from danger.

water. She does not know she could get her hand stuck. You need to keep her from playing in the toilet.

Keeping your child safe is a big job. You can help your child by keeping your house safe. You should put away anything that could break and hurt your child. Do this **before** your child gets hurt. This is called "childproofing." It means you make your house safe **before** your child gets hurt. When you childproof your house, your child will not break things. She will not hurt herself. You will not have to yell "no" as much, either.

Also, never leave a young child at home or in the car alone. Do not leave her even for a few minutes. Bad things happen fast. If there is a fire or medical problem, your child must have a responsible adult or caregiver there to help. Be sure that you know your child's caregiver well. Do not leave your child with anyone you think might hurt her if that person gets mad. And if you take your child to child care, check to make sure it is a healthy and safe place.

Being safe at home and away is important. When you are in a car, everyone must wear a seatbelt. (It's the law in the United States.) Never have more people in a car than you have seatbelts. If your child is under 4 years old, put her in a car seat.

Remember these tips:

- Always use the child safety seat.

- If your child is younger than 1 years old or weighs less than 25 pounds, face the seat backwards. If she is 1 year old or older or weighs more then 25 pounds, face it forward.

- Strap the car seat to the car with the seat belt. Make sure it fits tightly. You may need a seat belt safety clip. Check your car's manual or the safety seat manual to see if you need to use this clip.

- Strap your child to the car seat

Making Your Home Safe Chart

Read this list. Then go through your home, doing what has not been done. Put a check in each box as you do it.

Living Room

❑ Cover electrical outlets with plastic outlet covers (you can buy these in most stores).

❑ Take away small rugs so your child will not trip, or put rubber pads under them so the rugs do not slip.

❑ Put padding on the sharp edges of the table (use foam pads). If you cannot pad the table or do not want to, remove the table until your child is older.

❑ Some plants are poisonous. Put them on a high shelf that your child cannot reach.

❑ Cords on drapes should be short. Your child should not be able to reach them (if there are loops on cords, cut them).

❑ Put away anything that can break.

❑ Check all shelves and things your child can climb on. The shelves should be strong and not fall over.

❑ Put a screen in front of the fireplace and teach your child that this is not a place to play in. Put padding over the sharp edges of the hearth.

Kitchen

❑ Take knobs off the stove.

❑ Put sharp knives in a safe place.

❑ Put matches in a safe place.

❑ When you are cooking, try to use only the back burners. Turn pan handles in so your child cannot reach them and pull the pots off the stove.

❑ Put all cleaners, paints, and detergents in a cabinet with a child safety lock (you can buy a child safety lock in most stores).

❑ Do not use cleaners near your child (the smell can make him sick or burn his skin).

❑ If your child swallows poison, call Poison Control immediately. Have "Syrup of Ipecac" ready in case Poison Control tells you to give it to him (you can buy "Syrup of Ipecac" in the drugstore).

❑ Unplug everything when you are not using it (toaster, iron, blender, and so on).

❑ Keep all plastic bags and garbage bags in a safe place away from your child.

❑ Wipe up all spilled liquid from the floor. Do this right when it happens.

Bathroom

❑ Keep caps on all bottles. Always use the safety caps.

❑ Lock up all medicines (aspirin, alcohol, laxatives and so on).

❑ Put rubber mats in the bath tub or shower.

❑ Keep a bath mat next to the bath tub and shower.

❑ Put a toilet lid latch on the toilet if your child likes to reach in.

❑ If you can, lower the temperature of your hot water heater to 120° F at the most. The hot water should not be able to burn your hand. If you cannot change the water temperature, use a hot water faucet guard (you can buy a hot water faucet guard in most stores). Be sure your faucets cannot be turned on easily.

** Important: **Never** leave a child alone in the bath tub.

★ Note: You may be able to borrow or buy cheaply a car seat from a public healthcare organization. Ask around!

Child's Bedroom

❑ Look at all toys. Take away all toys with broken or sharp edges. Also take away toys with pieces smaller than a big walnut.

❑ Use only toys that are right for your child's age.
❑ Make sure windows cannot open.
❑ Cover electrical outlets.

Stairs

❑ If you have a young child, put a gate at the top and bottom of the stairs.

❑ If you have an older child, keep stairs clear of toys, papers, and other objects.

Garage or Workroom

❑ Put away all tools so your child cannot reach them.
❑ Put paints and other poisons in a safe place, out of reach.

❑ Lock up all poisons.
❑ Put nails and screws in a safe place, out of reach.

Laundry Room

❑ Always close washing machine and dryer doors.

❑ Keep detergents and fabric softeners out of reach.

Other Things to Check

❑ Window blind cords should be short
❑ Garbage cans should be kept in a locked closet or high off the floor.
❑ Cover all electrical outlets.
❑ Have smoke alarms in the house. Check them every month. Change the batteries twice a year when the time changes.
❑ Have fire extinguishers in the house and know how to use them.

❑ Practice how to get out of the house if there is a fire. Remember to crawl on the floor. Have an escape plan.
❑ Put these numbers by your telephone: poison control, fire, police, emergency medical services, pediatrician.
❑ Get a child safety car seat for riding in the car.

❑ _____

❑ _____

❑ _____

❑ _____

❑ _____

❑ _____

Playing Safe Chart

You can help your child keep safe by giving him safe toys. Here are some safe things your child can do:

Kitchen

❏ Let your child play in a low drawer. That will be her drawer. Put safe things, such as pots, pans, and cartons, in that drawer for her. She will have something safe to do when you are working in the kitchen.

Bathroom

❏ Keep a low drawer or box for your child here. Fill it with safe things.

❏ Put a low, safe stool in the bathroom for your child. Let him use it when he is learning to wash his hands. He can also use it when he brushes his teeth.

Bedroom or Living Room

❏ Make some low shelves for your child. You can use colorful plastic crates to hold the shelves. Use these shelves to store your child's toys. She will be able to see the toys here and will want to play with them more.

❏ Use a shoe box to store your child's small toys. Draw or cut out a picture of the toys. Then glue it on the shoe box. Your child will learn that all the farm animals will go in the box with the picture of the farm animals on it. The blocks will go in the box with the picture of the blocks on it.

❏ When your child no longer puts things in her mouth, have a basket of magazines your child can use. Let her tear them, cut them, or color them. These magazines are just for her.

❏ Put up a low hook with a blunt, plastic end. Your child can hang up his coat or sweater there.

❏ Put a basket in your child's room. Teach him to put his dirty clothes in the basket.

List your own safety ideas and concerns about your child's toys and play areas.

─────────── **Other Ideas for Playing Safe:** ───────────

_____

_____

_____

_____

_____

_____

_____

_____

_____

_____

_____

_____

_____

_____

_____

_____

_____

_____

_____

_____

Build a Bond with Your Child

What Is a "Bond"?

A bond with your child is a special connection. Even though you cannot see it, you **can** feel it with your heart when the bond is strong. It is a special feeling you have for your child. When you have a strong bond, you want to protect your child and teach him to be a responsible person. Your child wants to do things for you, too.

The bond starts when your child is born. As your child grows, the bond becomes stronger or weaker. When you are "too hard" or "too soft" as a parent, the bond becomes weaker. When you use the "just right" style, the bond becomes stronger. You build a strong bond when you give your child love and respect. The bond also grows when you have fun with your child.

It is easier to teach your child when you have a strong bond. He will listen to you and obey your rules. He will like to be near you because he knows you love him. He will want to talk with you when he has a problem.

You build a strong bond when you play with your child a little every day.

Here are some ways you can build a stronger bond with your child:

Every Day, a Little Play

This is a fun thing to do. You build a strong bond when you play and laugh with your child.

26

When you play with your child you:

- Build her self-esteem

- Help her learn about the world

- Help her learn new skills

Playing with a 1-year-old is different than playing with a 4-year-old. Each child at each stage will be different. On the next page there is a list of games you can play with your child at each age. You can also make up your own games. Your child may have a game she loves to play over and over again.

When you have a busy day, you can find time to play while doing other things such as driving, buying groceries, or giving your child a bath. Making things fun will help your child want to do these things, too!

Play with your child every day. Playing with your child a few minutes a day is better than playing once a week for 1 hour. You can learn to play and enjoy your child's laughter.

What games do you and your child enjoy playing now?

_____

_____

_____

_____

_____

_____

_____

_____

Playing to Learn Chart

Here are some more games that fit your child's age and stage.

	Age 1 to 1 1/2	Age 1 1/2 to 2	
Blocks	All kinds of blocks. Children will put them on top of each other and knock them down. **Your child learns how to use her hands and feet. She learns what happens when you hit the blocks.**	All kinds of blocks. Your child will stack them up tall or put them in a long line. **Your child learns to build things and put things in order.**	
Books	Picture books of animals, buildings, trucks, and other things he sees every day. Books with rhymes are good, too. (Your librarian can show you which books children at different ages like.) **Your child learns the sounds of words and learns to listen.**	Picture books of animals, buildings, and different places. Nursery rhyme books are good, too. **Your child learns to talk and listen. She learns new words like "in," "out," "over," "under."**	
Music	Simple songs and singing nursery rhymes. **Your child learns to listen and to make sounds. She learns how words sound with music.**	Simple songs and playing with your fingers. **Your child learns new sounds and rhythm.**	
Objects	Plastic bowls or cups, lids, buckets, blocks. **Your child learns how each part works. He learns that some things fit into other things, and some things fit on top of other things.**	Simple puzzles, things he can fill up or empty, things with different shapes. **Your child learns how to use his hands better. He understands the words "inside" and "outside."**	
Pretend	Dolls, stuffed animals, old clothes, hats, blankets. **Your child learns how to act and how other people or animals act.**	A toy telephone, toy vacuum cleaner, pots and pans, other pretend adult items. **Your child learns how to imagine and how adults act.**	
Touch and Feel Things	Tubs filled with water, soft cloth, sticky things, cold things, sand. **Your child learns more about his world through feeling and touching.**	Tubs with water, buckets or cups he can fill up or empty, sand, rice. **Your child learns more about hard and soft, wet and dry, empty and full.**	

Age 2 to 2 1/2	Age 3	Age 4
Large wooden blocks, big Legos with little people, animals, cars. **Your child learns to think and create.**	Small square blocks to make towers, large blocks to make roads, buildings or tunnels. **Your child learns to balance things and think about how the world works.**	All sizes of blocks and boxes, toys with different shapes that fit together. **Your child learns to plan and build. He learns how to solve problems.**
Simple, short stories with a beginning, a middle, and an end. **Your child learns to talk and listen. She will learn to tell stories with new words.**	Books with pictures and 2 or 3 sentences on each page. **Your child learns to recognize letters. This will also help her learn to read later.**	Silly and funny books, rhyming book, stories about children or animals, stories that are about simple problems. **Your child learns that people read from left to right. She learns that words and letters have different sounds.**
Songs, playing with your fingers, drums you make. **Your child learns to practice new words and sounds. He learns to follow directions.**	Songs with motion. **Your child learns to use words, sound, and his body together.**	Children's songs; pots, pans, boxes, drums, and other things to make noise with. **Your child learns that songs have rhythm. She learns that her voice has different tones.**
Play-dough, plastic cookie cutters, rolling pin, balls, large cardboard boxes. **Your child learns to think about what he is doing.**	Puzzles with 8 or 10 large pieces, bright beads that snap together, things with different shapes. **Your child learns how things fit together, how colors look together, and how to put things in order.**	Small beads to string together, children's scissors, puzzles. **Your child learns to make hands and eyes work together. He learns to work slowly and carefully.**
Dolls, doll clothes, empty food boxes, mail you do not want. **Your child learns how adults act.**	Toy telephone, toy dishes, old clothes. **Your child learns about adults by acting like adults.**	Old clothes, dolls, doll clothes, puppets, masks, costumes. **Your child learns that some things are pretend and some things are real.**
Helping you cook simple things. **Your child learns about hot and cold, sticky, wet, soft and how to follow directions.**	Finger paints, clay, colored markers, and markers that have different smells. **Your child learns to use her hands, fingers, and her mind to make different things.**	Water and sand with pails and shovels, plastic tubes, art supplies. **Your child learns that she can make things happen. She learns how things feel and how they move.**

Taking Care of Yourself

Taking time to take care of yourself is a good way to keep your energy up.

You have a big job taking care of your children. But who takes care of you? You do. That is part of your job as a parent. When you take good care of yourself, you will have energy and will feel happier. This will help you take care of your child.

Taking care of yourself is called "self-care." Self-care means that you get enough sleep, eat healthy food, and do things that make you happy. This helps keep you fresh and healthy. Your child needs you this way.

Each day you give a lot of energy to other people and your children. You need to give yourself some energy, too. But can you give yourself too much care? Yes. Some parents spend too much time taking care of themselves. They do not give enough to their children. Other parents give too much to their children. They do not have enough energy for themselves. When you are a "just right" parent, you give time to your children **and** to yourself.

Here are some ways you can give yourself self-care:

- Healthy body

- Healthy mind

- Talk and visit with other people

- Get organized

Self-Care Chart

Healthy body:

1. Eat healthy food.
2. Do not drink a lot of alcohol.
3. Get enough sleep.
4. Exercise.

5._____
6._____
7._____
8._____
9._____
10._____

Talk and visit with other people:

1. Talk with other parents once a week.
2. Spend time with your friends.
3. Find someone to talk to about problems.

4._____
5._____
6._____
7._____
8._____
9._____
10._____

Healthy mind:

1. When things get too wild, stop. Try to relax and be calm.
2. Spend time outdoors. Take a walk; go to the park; sit by a lake.
3. Relax! Take a bath, listen to music, or read.

4._____
5._____
6._____
7._____
8._____
9._____
10._____

Get organized:

1. Make a list each day of things you need to do.
2. Keep a calender to mark times and places where you have to be.
3. Take time to organize each part of your home.

4._____
5._____
6._____
7._____
8._____
9._____
10._____

Now choose 1 new self-care activity to do for yourself this week. Write this activity here.

I will do this for myself:

_____

_____

_____

_____

_____

Enjoy it! This is for you.

Home Activities

Things I will do before the next class:

❑ I will take care of myself. How?

_____

_____

❑ I will play with my child. How?

_____

_____

❑ I will make my home safer for my child. How?

_____

_____

❑ I will read Chapter 1 in this *Workbook* and complete the activities.

Do these 4 things at home this week.

How did you feel when you finished them?

After I gave myself some self-care, I felt:

_____

_____

_____

_____

_____

_____

After I played with my child, I felt:

_____

_____

_____

_____

_____

_____

This is what happened when I made my home safer for my child:

_____

_____

_____

_____

_____

_____

Notes:

CHAPTER 2

Preventing Problems

Teaching Your Child Is Important

How do you teach your child to share, take turns, and obey the rules? Children need to learn these things so they can work and cooperate with others. This will help them grow up healthy and happy. If they do not learn these things, they may be unhappy and may not enjoy life. But if you teach your children how to

Your children learn many things from you. Teaching them to behave and cooperate with others will help them throughout their lives.

behave, you will love to be around them, and so will other people!

We will suggest some ways to teach your child how to act responsibly. Our ways have worked for millions of parents. They will work for you, too. But it will take time and practice. Do not stop if these ways do not work the first time. Keep trying them, and your children will change. You may be doing some things now that work with your child. Good for you! Or you may decide not to use some of our ways. That's OK. You are the parent, and you should decide.

Discipline

All children misbehave sometimes. They are learning about the world, about you, and about themselves. Sometimes they break your rules. Your job is to teach your child to learn without breaking the rules. Sometimes, young children think about themselves only. We want to teach them to think about other people sometimes and what they need. We also want to teach young children how to do more things themselves.

Teaching is sometimes called discipline. In fact, discipline means teaching. It does not mean hurting your children when they make you mad.

You should not:

- yell

- call them names

- use bad language

- shake them

- hit them or spank them

This hurts children. It can harm their bodies, and it hurts their feelings. It also hurts the bond you are building with your child. It can even teach your child to misbehave more! Your parents may have treated you this way. But you do not have to treat your child this way.

You can choose to teach your child in better ways. You can choose to show love and respect for your child.

Getting Your Child to Come When You Call

Parents hate it when children do not come when they are called. For example, pretend your child is playing with his toys. You say, "It is time for dinner. Come to the table." But your child does not move. He pretends he does not hear you. So you get angry and say, "Come to the table, now!" But your child still does not move. Now both of you are angry and upset.

You may think your child is misbehaving. That may be true. But there is something else that is happening, too. When children start doing something, they have a hard time stopping. We want them to stop when we say stop. If they do not stop, we get angry. But they are not trying to make us angry. They just need some time to change what they are doing. They need some time to finish their play and change to something else. When we talk about this problem, we say, "Children have lousy brakes." They take a long time to slow down and stop.

You can help your child by giving her time to get ready to stop her play.

For example, you can say, "Dinner will be ready soon. You have only a few minutes to finish what you are doing."

Then wait 3 or 4 minutes and say, "Dinner is almost ready. Please stop what you are doing. Come and wash your hands."

Some parents say, "OK. You have 2 minutes to stop. Then you have to wash your hands for dinner."

Remember that your young child cannot tell time. But he will learn how long 2 minutes is soon when you try this method. Some children like it when you use the kitchen timer. Set the timer for 5 or 10 minutes. Tell them that they will need to stop when the timer rings. For example, say, "I will set the timer for 5 minutes. Try to put your socks and shoes on before it rings."

Some parents let their children have "1 more time" before they have to stop.

Example: "You can go down the slide 1 more time. Then we go home."

Be careful that you do what you say. "One more time" means 1 time and not 10 times. Use this way to teach your child how to slow down, and she will behave better and better.

Choices give children power to decide some things for themselves.

The Power of Choice

Another way you can help teach your child is to give her choices. Children want to decide some things for themselves. They do not want their parents to always tell them what to do. They also will say "no" a lot if you do not give them a chance to think and make choices.

You can give your child choices. This will help her grow and think. But she should not be free to make **any** choice. You decide what choices to give her.

For example, here is a parent giving **no choice**:

Parent: "Here is your orange juice. Drink it."
Child: "No, I hate it."

Here is a parent **giving a choice:**

Parent: "Would you like to have orange juice or apple juice this morning?"
Child: "Apple juice."

You teach your child when you give choices. You teach her to think, and you teach her that she can make choices. It gives her power.

Tips for Giving Choices

1. Give only 2 choices at a time. Young children are not ready for many choices. For example, ask, "Would you like corn flakes or oatmeal this morning?" Do not ask, "What do you want for breakfast?"

2. The choices should be OK with you. Do not give a choice of oatmeal or pancakes if you do not want to make pancakes. Also, give choices that are safe and healthy for your child's age.

3. Do not make everything a choice. Making choices is hard work. Do not give your child a lot of choices. It may be too much for her. Sometimes she just wants you to tell her what to choose.

Choices Worksheet

Write 3 commands you give your child which you could say as choices. You might think of problem areas such as bedtime or dressing. Then re-write these commands as choices.

Command:	Choice:

Example:

Put on this shirt.   Would you like to wear this white shirt or the red one?

1._____

_____

2._____

_____

3._____

Give these choices to your child this week.

After you try them, write down what happened.

How did your child act?

1._____

_____

2._____

_____

3._____

_____

The When-Then Rule

This rule will help you get your child to do something that she does not want to do. Here is how it works. You tell your child that **when** she does what you want her to do, **then** she can do what she wants to do.

For example, Bobby does not like to take a bath. He says "no" every night. But Bobby does like to listen to music with Mom. So his mother says, "Bobby, **when** you take your bath, **then** you can listen to music with me." He chooses to take a bath because he wants to listen to music. That is the When-Then rule.

The When-Then rule helps you get your child to do something she does not want to do.

When-Then Rule Tips

When you use this rule remember:

1. Do not give a special reward for the choice.
What your child gets to do should be something he usually does and likes. For example, Bobby usually listens to music after he takes his bath.

If you give a special reward, such as toys or candy, your child will always expect it. This will cause problems later.

2. Always say "when . . . , then . . . ." For example:

- **"When** you put all your cars in the box, **then** we can go get a snack."

- **"When** you get your coat on, **then** we can go to the park."

3. Be firm and friendly when you use the rule. If your voice is "too hard" or "too soft," the rule will not work as well.

4. Look at your child when you talk to her. You may need to get on the floor to be close to her. Your eye-to-eye contact gets your child's attention. It also lets her know you mean what you say.

When-Then Rule Worksheet

Are you having a problem with your child? Do you have a hard time getting her to do something? Write that on the line below:

Example: <u>Getting Ben to take his bath.</u>

Your Problem:

_____

_____

_____

_____

What will you say to your child the next time you have this problem? Think of what your child likes to do.

Example:
When <u>you have taken your bath,</u>

Then <u>we can listen to your music together.</u>

When_____

Then_____

Try this at home with your child.

After you try it, write down what happened here.

_____

_____

_____

_____

The ACT* Rule

The When-Then rule is great for getting your child to start doing something. But how do you teach your child to *stop* doing something?

The ACT rule has 3 steps. It helps you give your child a positive choice.

For example: "How can I teach Tanya not to play with her food?"
You can use the **ACT rule.** It has 3 steps:

Step 1: <u>A</u>ccept your child's wishes or feelings.

Tell her it is OK for her to want something. Let her know you understand how she feels. This does not mean you give her what she wants. It means you understand her feelings.

For example: "I know you like to touch and feel things." We call this: <u>A</u>ccept your child's wishes or feelings.

Step 2: Communicate the rule.

Tell your child the rules. Let her know that you understand how she feels, but you do not like how she acts. Be calm when you speak to her. Tell her that the way she is acting is not OK. Tell her the right way to act.

For example: "We do not play with food. We eat food." We call this: Communicate the rule.

Step 3: Target a positive choice.

After you tell your child what she cannot do, give her another choice. Give her something else she **can** do. Help her find a better way to get her wish.

For example: "After you finish your lunch, I have some colorful dough that you can poke and mash." We call this: Target a positive choice.

Young children may stop what they are doing if there is something new to do. They like new things.

Let's look at some more examples:

For example:

Step 1:	Accept your child's wishes or feelings.	"I know you like jumping on the bed."
Step 2:	Communicate the rule.	"But beds are for sleeping, not jumping. We might fall off and get hurt."
Step 3:	Target a positive choice.	"We can line up some pillows on the floor for you to jump on now. After I do my work, we can go outside and play."

For example:

Step 1: <u>A</u>ccept your child's wishes or feelings.

"I am glad you like to play basketball. It looks like you are having fun."

Step 2: <u>C</u>ommunicate the rule.

"But we do not play ball inside our home."

Step 3: <u>T</u>arget a positive choice.

"I will take you outside later. Right now we can set up a little hoop in your room. You can use the foam ball Uncle Jack gave you. Use that when you play in the house."

For example:

Step 1: <u>A</u>ccept your child's wishes or feelings.

"I know you are angry with me."

Step 2: <u>C</u>ommunicate the rule.

"But we do not scream at each other."

Step 3: <u>T</u>arget a positive choice.

"You can go scream in your room. When you feel calmer, we can talk about what is upsetting you."

Sometimes you do not have time to think of the steps in the right order.

For example, Pete, a 2-year-old, is chewing on a balloon. His dad remembers that many children die when balloons get caught in their throats. So he needs to act fast. He takes the balloon out of Pete's mouth and says, "No. We do not put balloons in our mouths. They can pop and get caught in your throat. I know you like to taste things. But balloons are not safe for you. Let me put this away. I will get you a cracker that you can eat."

Pete's father used the ACT rule and said all the steps. He just said them in the wrong order. That's OK if something dangerous is about to happen. At other times, try to use the steps in the A-C-T order.

ACT Rule Tips

All these ways you can use to teach your child will work if you "walk your talk." What does that mean? Children watch what we do more than what we say. Do you do what you say you will do? If you do, then your child will listen to you. Here are 3 things that will help you walk your talk:

1. Look your child in the eyes when you talk to him. You may need to get on your knees to look at him. Or you may need to hold him on your lap and look at his face. When you talk to him this way, he will hear you better.

2. Show your child another choice. For example, if Pete sees the cracker, he will give Dad the balloon. If Maggie sees the foam ball, she will give up the hard ball.

3. You may have to move the child. If your child does not stop what she is doing, what do you do? You should move her. You can do this by gently lifting under her arms. Point her in another direction. If she will not move, stay calm and gentle. Give her a choice.

For example, ask, "Do you want to walk by yourself or do you want me to carry you?"

If she does not move on her own, pick her up and say, "I guess you want me to carry you."

If she screams and cries, take her to her room or to another quiet place. Tell her when she stops crying and yelling, then she can come out and play. After about 2 to 4 minutes, ask her if she is ready to stop crying and come out. If she says yes, give her a hug. But if she still cries, tell her you will come back later. Check again in 2 to 4 minutes, and then every 5 to 10 minutes.

ACT Rule Worksheet

Are you having a problem with your child? What do you want him or her to stop doing? Write it below:

─────────── **Problem #1** ───────────

_____

_____

Now write what you will say in the next 3 steps:

Step 1: **A**

I know you like to_____

_____

Step 2: **C**

But_____

_____

Step 3: **T**

How about _____

_____

─────────── **Problem #2** ───────────

_____

_____

Step 1: **A** _____

Step 2: **C** _____

Step 3: **T** _____

What happened when you tried this at home with your child?

_____

_____

Children Need Rules

Often children misbehave because they do not know how to act. They need to learn. And they will learn if we teach them the right way to act. Making rules is one way to teach them. When they follow the rules, they learn how to get along. And making good rules will help you prevent many problems. Then when your children grow up, they will know how to act their best.

Why do we make rules?

1. We have rules to keep our children safe. Children do not know about the world. They do not know it can be dangerous. We make rules to keep our children safe.

Rules help keep children safe. Rules also help them get along with others.

For example:

- Rule: Children do not play with knives.
- Rule: We wear a coat when it is cold outside.

2. We have rules to protect other people. Children can hurt adults and other children.

For example:

- Rule: We do not bite people.
- Rule: We do not hit people.

3. We have rules to help children make choices. They do not know how to make all of their choices. Rules help them when they are not old enough to decide.

For example:

- Rule: Children can watch only the movies parents choose. (They are not ready to watch all movies. Some are too scary or violent.)
- Rule: We eat sweets only after we eat our dinner. (It is not healthy for children to eat sweets instead of healthy food.)

4. We have rules to make parenting easier. You should not have to think of what to do each time something happens. Instead, you can apply a rule. Plus, if your child knows your rules, he will misbehave less.

For example:

- Rule: We do not eat food in the bedroom.
- Rule: Dirty clothes go in the hamper.

Tips for Making Rules

1. Make only the rules you really need. It is hard for young children to remember a lot of rules. Older children can remember more. At first, rules about health and safety are the most important. You might wait until your child is 4 or 5 years old before you teach rules about manners.

2. Give 1 rule at a time. Keep it short and simple.

3. Make rules that sound fair.

For example, say, "Bedtime for children in our home is at 8:00." This sounds like a rule for all children.

Do not say, "You have to go to bed at 8:00." This sounds like it is a rule for that night only.

For example, say, "We eat our food only in the kitchen."

Do not say, "You cannot take food out of the kitchen." When the rule sounds fair, your child will follow it more often.

4. Say the rule in a positive way.

For example, say: "We sit on sofas. Please sit down."

Do not say only, "Do not jump on the sofa." Remember, children behave better when they know what to do.

5. Tell your child the rule in a firm but calm voice. Get close to your child. Look into her face.

6. Repeat the rule if your child breaks it. But what happens if she breaks the rule again? Use a consequence to correct her. (You will learn about consequences in Chapter 3.)

Always enforce your rules. If you ignore them sometimes, your child will think the rules are not important.

7. Encourage your child when he remembers a rule. Give him a smile or a hug. Show him you know he is acting responsibly. Soon he will feel good about your rules.

Encourage your child with a hug or positive word when she remembers your rule. Then she will feel good about following the rule again.

Making Rules Worksheet

Does your child misbehave sometimes? What does he or she do?
Write it below.

Problem:

_____

_____

Now write a rule for this problem.

Rule:_____

_____

Next, check your rule with these questions:

❑   Do you really need this rule?
❑   Is the rule short and simple?
❑   Does it sound like it is a fair rule?
❑   Is the rule positive?

The next time your child misbehaves, tell him the rule.

Did you say the rule in a firm and calm voice?_____

Did your child obey the rule?_____

If "yes," did you encourage her? How?_____

_____

If "no," did you do what you said you would do if he broke the rule?

_____

_____

Then what happened?

_____

_____

Build a Bond with a Routine

Do you do some things each day at the same time? This is called a routine. Children love routines! They love to do the same things the same way over and over. They want to know some things will happen again and again. Routines help children to feel safe and secure. Here are some routines that may help you:

Morning routine:
❑ Do your children wake up the same time each morning?

❑ Do they wash, brush their teeth, and get dressed in the same order?

❑ Do they eat breakfast at the same time each morning?

Eating routine:
❑ Do they eat lunch and dinner at about the same time each day?

Daily routines, such as bathtime, can have plenty of fun built in!

❑ Do they eat in the same place each day?

Sleeping routine:
❑ Do they take a nap each day?

❑ Do they take a nap the same time each day?

❑ Do they do the same things each night before they go to bed?

❑ Do they go to bed at the same time each night?

A routine will help your child learn how to act, and it will teach your child the rules. It will also help your child feel secure. If you make each routine fun, your child will learn to enjoy each day. (Remember, you can change a routine if another one is better.)

Here are some examples of routines:

Morning routine

6:00   Mother wakes up. She gets herself ready.

6:30   Mother wakes up Lisa, her 3-year-old. She gently kisses Lisa on the cheek. She says, "Time to get up, Lisa."

6:31   Mother turns on a lamp. She takes some clothes out of the closet. She says, "Lisa, do you want to wear this red shirt or that blue shirt?"

6:35   Mother helps Lisa get dressed. She lets Lisa do as much as she can.

6:45   Mother makes breakfast. First she asks Lisa what kind of cereal she wants that day. Then she pours juice for them both.

7:05   Mother takes Lisa to the bathroom. She helps her brush her teeth and wash her face. She brushes her hair.

7:15   Mother and Lisa get in the car. Mother drives to day care.

What is your morning routine?

Time	Activity

Sleeping routine (for naps during the day)

2:00   Mother and Joey, her 2-year-old, get in a rocking chair to read a story.

2:15   The story is finished. Mother plays soft music or sings softly to Joey. She rocks him.

2:20   Mother puts Joey in the bed. She says, "Sleep well, sweetheart. I love you."

4:00   Joey wakes up and calls for his mother. Mother comes into the bedroom. She says, "Did you have a good nap?" She picks him up and says, "Would you like some juice?" They go to the kitchen and have some juice.

What is your sleeping routine?

Time	Activity

Bedtime Routine

7:30   Father fills the bathtub. He tells Daniel, his 4-year-old, to take his clothes off.

7:35   Father gives Daniel a bath. He plays some fun music. He puts 2 or 3 toys in the bathtub for his son. He plays with Daniel before he starts to wash him. (Note: Never leave a young child alone in the bathtub. He may drown!)

7:45   Father dries Daniel and helps him put on his pajamas. Father flosses and brushes Daniel's teeth. Then Father helps his son brush his own teeth and comb his hair.

7:55   Father reads Daniel a story.

8:05   Father and son say a prayer. Father says, "I love you, son." Daniel says, "I love you, too." Father turns off the light and leaves the door open, just a little. (Note: Your child should sleep in his own bed, if possible. If he gets scared at night and gets in your bed, take him back to his bed and comfort him. Stay for a little while and then say "Goodnight.")

Write a bedtime routine that you can use with your child:

Time	Activity

Build a Bond with 3 Little Words

You cannot tell your child "I love you" too many times!

All children love to hear the words, "I love you." Your children need to hear these words from you, too. Tell them you love them each day. Tell them when they take a nap. Tell them before they go to bed at night. Tell them many times during the day. Watch them smile when they hear the words. They love it. You cannot give your child too much love. You cannot spoil your child with love, either.

"I Love You" Worksheet

When did you say "I love you" to your child this week?

_____

_____

Where were you?

_____

_____

What did your child say?

_____

_____

How did you feel?

_____

_____

Taking Care of Yourself

Remember that an important part of parenting "just right" is taking good care of yourself. Turn back to your list of self-care ideas on page 31. Add any new ideas you have learned. Then choose 2 ideas to do and write them below.

Self-care activity #1:

_____

Self-care activity #2:

_____

After you do your 2 self-care activities, fill in below.

After self-care #1 I felt: _____

_____.

How did this help you be a better parent?

_____

_____

_____

_____

After self-care #2 I felt: _____

_____.

How did this help you be a better parent?

_____

_____

_____

_____

Home Activities

Here is a list of things for you to do this week. Check the box after you have done them:

❑ Do something for yourself

❑ Remember to say, "I love you" to your child

❑ Use the When-Then rule

❑ Use the ACT rule

❑ Play with your child

❑ Read Chapter 2 of this *Workbook* and finish the activities.

How did you feel when you finished them?

After I said "I love you" to my child, I felt:

_____

_____

_____

_____

_____

After I used the When-Then rule, I felt:

_____

_____

_____

_____

_____

After I used the ACT rule, this happened:

_____

_____

_____

_____

_____

_____

After I played with my child, I felt:

_____

_____

_____

_____

_____

_____

When you encourage your child, you build a lifelong bond.

Notes:

CHAPTER 3

Encouraging Positive Behavior

Temperament

Think back to when you were growing up. Did you live with a brother or sister? Did you act like your brother or sister? No. You acted like you. All children go through the same ages and stages. But they do not act the same. **Temperament** is one of the things that makes each child act differently. **Temperament** means the personality traits that we are born with. Every child has a different temperament.

Temperament Checklist

Choose one of your children for this list. Put his or her name at the top of the list. Then check each box that describes this child.

Name

_____

What is her energy level?
- ❑ High energy
- ❑ Medium energy
- ❑ Low energy

How does she feel about change?
- ❑ Likes changes
- ❑ Can accept changes
- ❑ Does not like changes

Every child acts differently, even brothers. Each is born with his or her own temperament.

How does she feel about other people?
- ❑ Enjoys people and likes to play with other children
- ❑ Sometimes enjoys people; sometimes likes to play by herself
- ❑ Likes to play by herself

What are your child's feelings?

❏ Usually happy, pleasant

❏ Is sometimes happy, sometimes sad

❏ Often either unhappy or sad

What is your child's will-power like?

❏ Strong-willed; likes to lead

❏ Medium-willed

❏ Gentle; likes to follow

How is your child organized?

❏ Likes to be very neat

❏ Is neat sometimes

❏ Is usually messy

All of these temperaments are normal. They all have benefits, too. For example, does your child have high energy and a strong will? She may be hard to live with. But she may also use these same traits to become a leader when she grows up.

Or does your child have low energy? He probably acts cranky when he has to do many things in one day. But he also may like to play by himself quietly when he can.

You can help your child work with his or her temperament. To do that, you will need to know your child and learn what she needs from you.

Temperament Tips

Check your child's traits. Then read how you can help your child work with that trait.

❏ Has high energy:

Your child needs a lot of OK ways to use her energy. Take her to the playground or some place where she can run and jump and make noise. Give her pots and pans or toys she can swing, throw, or kick.

❑ Has low energy:

Your child may get tired easily. Let her play quietly. She can read, draw pictures or watch movies. You can slowly help her play with more energy as she grows.

❑ Likes changes:

Your child enjoys going from one activity to another. She likes to go to new places and try new things. Help her also learn to stick with an activity for a little longer.

❑ Does not like changes:

Your child likes to stick with daily routines. Help her learn to try new things. Do not force her, but encourage her to explore.

❑ Enjoys people:

Your child may talk to strangers. He will be very friendly to other people. You should watch him closely, since some strangers may be harmful.

❑ Likes to play by himself:

This child is shy. But he will talk to people when he knows them. Tell your child about new people before he meets them. Help him play with others.

❑ Is happy, pleasant:

This child may be easy to live with as he is; enjoy him.

❑ Is often unhappy or sad:

Help your child look at the happy side of life. Point out the good things that happen, even when these things are small!

❑ Has a strong will; likes to lead:

Give this child lots of times to be the boss. Also give this child choices to make instead of orders to take. Help her cooperate with others.

❑ Is gentle; likes to follow:

Your child may be kind to others. You might need to help this child be stronger. For example, if someone takes his toy, teach him how to ask for it.

❑ Likes to be very neat:

Teach this child how to relax and enjoy life. He does not need to always have everything neat and in place.

❑ Is usually messy:

Help your child to be neater. Teach him to pick up toys and put away clothes.

You can help your child with his temperment. For example, you can help a messy child be neater.

Notes_____

_____

_____

_____

_____

Temperament Worksheet

This chart will help you learn more about your temperament and your child's temperament.

Put an **X** where you are. Put a ♥ where your child is.

For example, if most of the time you have high energy, and your child has low energy, you would mark the chart like this:

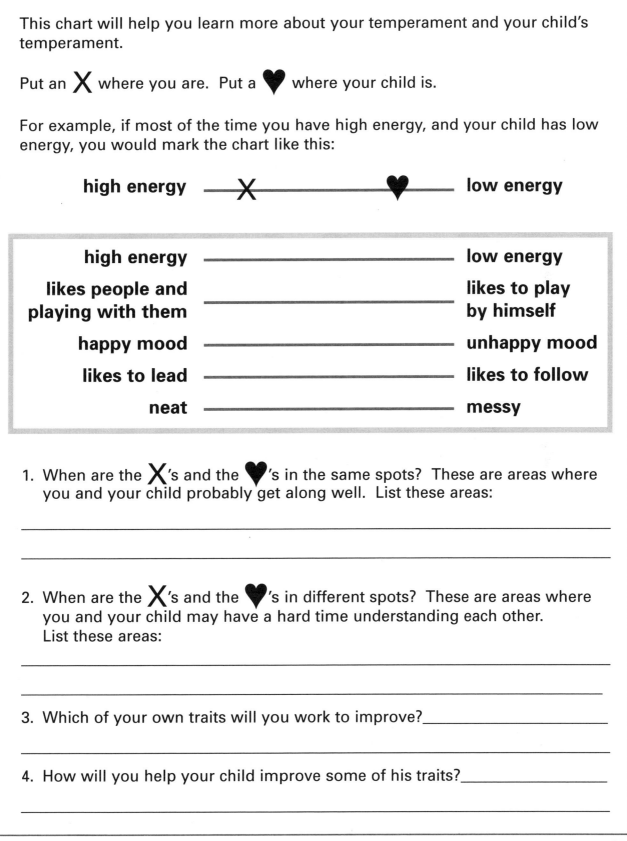

high energy —— X ———— ♥ —— **low energy**

high energy ————————————	**low energy**
likes people and playing with them ————————————	**likes to play by himself**
happy mood ————————————	**unhappy mood**
likes to lead ————————————	**likes to follow**
neat ————————————	**messy**

1. When are the **X**'s and the ♥'s in the same spots? These are areas where you and your child probably get along well. List these areas:

   _____

   _____

2. When are the **X**'s and the ♥'s in different spots? These are areas where you and your child may have a hard time understanding each other. List these areas:

   _____

   _____

3. Which of your own traits will you work to improve?_____

   _____

4. How will you help your child improve some of his traits?_____

   _____

Consequences

Children learn from consequences when they are connected to the misbehavior.

We want to help our children learn how to behave in positive ways. This may mean helping a child who has lots of energy learn not to run inside your home. Or, it may mean helping a child who does not follow rules to learn to follow them. It may mean taking the time to teach a child respect and how to be polite. But how do you do all this?

We can use many of the methods from Chapter 2. For example, we can make good rules and use the When-Then rule and the ACT rule. Even so, children will still misbehave sometimes.

When your child misbehaves, do you yell, hit, or shake him? This is not good for you or your child. It will not teach him how to act. There is a better way to teach children. It is called **consequences**. Each time we make a choice, something happens. The things that happen are called **consequences**. Your child will learn that each time she makes a choice, there will be a **consequence**.

Remember the ACT rule? Look at this example of a 2-year-old who hits his mother:

Step 1: <u>A</u>ccept your child's wishes or feelings.	"Son, I know you feel angry."
Step 2: <u>C</u>ommunicate the rule.	"In our family, we do not hit people."
Step 3: <u>T</u>arget a positive choice.	"How about hitting this pillow to show how mad you are?"

What happens if your son says, "No!" and hits you again? You can give him a choice. The child can behave, or he can do something that will help him learn how to behave. The second choice is the **consequence**.

For example, "You can stay here without hitting me or you can go to the bedroom to hit your pillow. It is your choice."

If he stops hitting, then he chose to behave. But if he hits you again, that means he chose the **consequence**. Then you gently tell him the **consequence.** You say, "I see you chose to go to the bedroom. Tell me when you are ready to come out and stay here without hitting." You take him by the hand and lead him to the bedroom.

What if your child hits again later? That is his choice. He will have the same **consequence**. Each time he hits you, you will take him to the bedroom. If you are in another place, take him away from the person he was hitting. He needs to learn that each time he hits there will be a consequence. The consequence is that he gets removed from the situation. Note: Do not hit him to punish him. You are trying to teach him not to hit, so you should not hit either.

Tips for Using Consequences

1. Consequences should be fair. You use a consequence to teach your child how to act. You do not use it to punish or hurt your child.

Example 1: Your child is playing a game of cards with you. He keeps throwing the cards around the room. You can give him a choice.

Good Choice:
"You can stop throwing the cards or you will have to stop playing the game."

Hurtful Choice:
"You can stop throwing the cards or you will get a spanking."

If he has to stop playing when he throws the cards, he will learn not to throw the cards. But if you spank him, he will just get mad. Spanking will only hurt him. It will not teach him to stop throwing the cards.

Example 2: Your child is playing with her food. You can give her a choice.

Good Choice:
"Stop playing with your food, or I will take your food away."

Hurtful Choice:
"Stop playing with your food, or you cannot watch TV tonight."

Think about the misbehavior. In this case, it is playing with food. Consequences work best when they fit the misbehavior. Taking the food away fits because he cannot play with it if it is gone. Keeping him from watching TV does not fit. Children learn best when the consequence fits.

Talk in a firm and calm voice when you discipline.

Example 3: You tell your child to put away his blocks. He does not listen to you. You can give him a choice:

Good Choice:
"Put your blocks away, or I will put them in a box in the closet."

Hurtful Choice:
"Put your blocks away, or you will have to stand in the corner for 5 minutes."

Not getting to play with the blocks fits the misbehavior. It teaches the child to take care of his things. Standing in the corner does not fit. It has nothing to do with the blocks.

2. Talk in a firm and calm voice. If you yell or are angry, he will only know you are mad. Then he may do it again to see if you get mad again. If you use a calm voice, he will listen to your words. This is the way to teach your child about consequences.

3. Give only those choices that are OK with you. You are the parent. You have a right to limit your child's choices to ones that you approve.

For example, Mother tells her 2-year-old son, Stephen, "Either stop biting or I will have to hold you so you cannot bite." Stephen tries to bite again, and Mother gets angry. She says, "I don't have time for this, Stephen!" Then she spanks him.

The mother gave her child a choice that was not OK with her. When her son chose to bite again, she got mad. She did not do what she said she would do. That is not fair.

Here is a better choice the mother could have used:

"Either play without biting or play alone in your crib, Stephen."

4. Give the choice one time. Then act! It is how you act that will teach your child. What happens when you give a choice and do not act? Your child learns to not listen to you. What happens when you give a choice one time and act? He will learn to listen to what you say.

For example, Megan and Ben like to play together. But sometimes one of them will hit the other. Father says, "Either play together without hitting, or you will each play alone in separate rooms." The next time he hears one of them yell "He hit me!" Father sends them to separate rooms for 10 minutes. After a few tries, Megan and Ben learn to play together without hitting.

Consequences Worksheet

Are you having a problem with your child? Write it in this space:

Problem _____

Write a **choice** and a **consequence** for your child:

Either_____

_____

Or_____

_____

Or you can write it this way:

When _____

_____

Then_____

_____

Use this choice and consequence the next time you have this problem with your child.

After you do it, fill in these blanks:

What happened? _____

Was your voice firm and calm? _____

How did your child act?_____

Did your child listen to you the first time? _____

Will you change how you act the next time?_____

Tantrums

When your child gets angry he may yell and cry. He may even fall on the floor and kick. This is called a **tantrum**. Many children have tantrums. They get angry when they do not get what they want. Your job is to teach your child how to manage his anger. Here are some tips that will help you:

1. Stay calm. If you get angry, your child will learn to do the same thing. Stay calm and think about what is happening.

2. Step back from her. When you are not there, she has no one to watch her yell and scream. You can say, "I cannot talk to you when you are crying and screaming. When you are finished, we will talk about it."

3. Talk gently. If you do not want to leave her alone, be gentle with her. Use a gentle voice. You can say, "It is OK. I know. You will be all right. I am here."

4. Hold her gently. Hold her with gentle arms until she is quiet. **Important:** This will work only if you hug and hold your child when she is happy, too. Do you hold her only when she has a tantrum? Then she will have a tantrum when she wants your love or hugs.

5. Do not give your child what he wants to get him to stop yelling and screaming. He will learn to have a tantrum to get his way. Wait until he has finished. Remember Step 3 of the ACT rule? You can help target a positive choice. You can say, "You cannot have a cookie now. It is almost time for dinner. You can have a cracker or some cheese."

6. Give a choice. Let your child have his tantrum where he is. Walk away from the area. But sometimes you cannot walk away. Your child may have a tantrum in front of other people. Say to your child, "Take some deep breaths and calm down, or you can scream in your room." You can gently carry him to his room. If you are in a store, take him outside until he is calm. If you have a car, put him in the car seat and sit quietly in your seat. Wait a few minutes. Then ask him, "Are you ready to be calm and go back inside?" Most children will be calm now. If he is not calm, wait a few minutes. Then ask him again.

Tips for Avoiding Tantrums

1. Make sure your child gets plenty of sleep. If she is tired, she will have tantrums more often. For example, is your child tired when you bring her shopping with you? Be sure she has a nap before you go out.

2. Make sure your child eats healthy food. Often children have tantrums when they are thirsty or hungry. So pack a healthy snack and juice when you go out together.

3. Let your child do things with you. Your child is interested in many things. If you go to the store, let him help you. He can put food in the cart. Talk to him, ask him questions, or give him something to do while you shop.

4. Find things your child can do in the house. Find things he can do for himself that are not too hard. If he is too young to button a shirt, get big buttons for him or something that snaps.

5. When your child goes out with you, bring along something fun. Bring a coloring book. Bring some crayons. Bring some small toys. Sing songs together while you are waiting. Play games together.

6. Use the ACT rule to help her find other good things to do. If he wants something he cannot have, help him find a choice he can have.

7. Tell him to take some deep breaths. This will help him calm down. When <u>you</u> are angry, take some deep breaths to calm down, too.

Tantrums Worksheet

Does your child have tantrums? When was the last tantrum?

_____

_____

_____

_____

Why did your child have a tantrum?

_____

_____

_____

_____

What did your child do when he or she was having the tantrum?

_____

_____

_____

_____

What did you do while your child was having the tantrum?

_____

_____

_____

_____

How can you help your child use his or her anger in a different way?

_____

_____

_____

_____

Encourage Your Children

When you **encourage** your children, you give them **courage**. You teach them how to live in this world without giving in to fear. Courage is the most important gift you can give your child. She will need to learn not to give up when she has a problem. She will need to learn to do the right thing even when it is hard. She will need courage to say "no" to drugs and other bad things. She will need courage to make her dreams come true.

You encourage your child when you tell her she is doing a good job.

Encourage means you build your child up. You help her see that she is doing a good job. You make her feel safe. You talk about the good things she does. This gives your child courage. Children need courage to grow just like plants need water to grow.

We **encourage** our children with helpful words and actions. We hug them. We listen to them. We help them when they need help. We leave them alone when they need quiet time. And when they make a mistake, we do not yell at them. We help them learn to do better.

Encouraging Tips

1. When your child needs your help, act. Do not walk away. Do not say, "I do not have time for you right now. Go play!" Your child needs courage to learn new things. And she learns when you help her. Take the time to teach her. She will learn to do things herself.

2. Help your child, but do not do everything for her. She will learn by doing things herself. She will learn by making mistakes. Let her make mistakes. When she finally does it right, she will feel very proud.

3. Help her learn 1 step at a time. Break big challenges down into small ones. Each time she does something right, she feels good. She has the courage to try to learn more new things.

For example, you can say, "I think you are big enough to learn to dress yourself. Do you want to learn to put on your shirt or pants?"

"You start putting on your shirt. I will help you if you need it."

"Let me show you how to put your dirty clothes in the basket."

4. Expect your child to behave well. Do not expect him to misbehave. If you think your child is bad, he will act bad. If you think your child will fail, he probably will fail. If you think your child is good and smart, he will act better.

For example, 4-year-old Doug is running in Grandma's home. He breaks a beautiful glass dish. Doug's mother gets angry and slaps him. She yells, "You are bad! I wish you were not born!"

Doug's mother was angry because Doug made a mistake. Then she said he was bad. Now he may think that he is bad. If he thinks he is bad, he will act bad. Really, he is a good child who made a mistake.

You are the most important person to your child. He believes everything you tell him. Your words and your actions help him to grow. If you believe in your child, he will believe in himself. You need to teach him to believe in himself.

Examples:
"You can do it. You are trying so hard!"

"You are a smart girl."

"Yea! You can dress yourself!"

"It may be hard, but you can do it."

"Running in Grandma's home was a mistake. You broke a dish and you felt bad. I bet next time you will remember to walk."

5. Notice what your child does right and talk about it. All children make mistakes. All children misbehave sometimes. Do you talk to your child only when he makes mistakes? Then he will make more mistakes to get your attention. Teach yourself to look at all the good things about your child. When was the last time you said, "Thank you" or "Good job" to your child?

Try to catch your child being good. Tell him that you are proud of him, and that you hope he is proud of himself.

For example, Father wants 3-year-old Jasmine to stay in bed at night after he puts her down. After 4 nights of getting out of bed many times, Jasmine gets up only 1 time. The next morning, Dad says, "You got out of bed only 1 time last night Jasmine. Good job! So tonight we'll have more time for a longer story."

For example, Mother wants her 2-year-old son, Kyle, to stop hitting when he is angry. She told him what to do when he is angry. She said he should talk about being angry.

One day Kyle wants to go outside to play. Mother says "We can't because it's raining outside." Then Kyle gets angry and says, "It is not fair!" Mother says, "I know you are angry. We can find something fun to do inside. I am glad you let me know you are angry by using words and not hitting. I like that."

When you want to encourage your child you can say:

"Nice job."

"I like that!"

"Thanks!"

"You were a great help."

"Wonderful!"

"You did a really good job."

"You looked happy when you did that!"

"I bet that felt good!"

"You look proud of yourself!"

"You are getting closer and closer—soon you can do this <u>all by yourself</u>!"

Expect the best from your child!

Encouragement Worksheet

1. What can you say and do when you are busy and your child needs your help?

_____

_____

_____

_____

2. What things do you do for your child that he could do for himself?

_____

_____

_____

_____

3. What words do you use when you are teaching your child something new?

_____

_____

_____

_____

4. What do you say to your child when you think she will make a mistake?

_____

_____

_____

_____

5. What can you say to your child to encourage her?

_____

_____

_____

_____

You Need Courage, Too

You need courage just like your child. Think of some good things about you and your child:

I am good at_____

_____

_____.

My child is good at _____

_____

_____.

People like me because _____

_____

_____.

I like my child because _____

_____

_____.

I am learning to _____

_____

_____.

My child is learning to _____

_____

_____.

Where You Can Go for Help

It is sometimes hard being a parent. But people in your community can help you. Here is a list of some people who may be able to help you and some places where you can go for help:

- your parents

- sisters, brothers, grandparents, aunts, uncles

- friends

- church or other place of worship

- your child's pre-school teacher or child-care worker

- your child's doctor or children's hospital

- books about parents

- other parents

Some of these people can tell you about places where you can get help. Some cost very little money, and some are free.

Can you think of places where you can go for help? Write them below:

_____

_____

_____

_____

_____

_____

_____

Your Child Needs You

Your child wants to grow up to be happy and healthy. But he needs you to teach him how. The most important person in your child's life is you.

We hope you have learned a lot from this book. Keep learning! Ask about more books you can read. And tell your friends about the *1, 2, 3, 4 Parents!* course. Tell them what you have learned and listen to what they know. Always listen to your heart and your child's heart. Together you will do what is right to be healthy and happy.

And remember to keep taking care of yourself, too. Your child needs you to take some time just for you. Do things that are healthy and that make you happy. Then when you do things for your child, you will be at your best.

Your parenting job is one of the most important jobs in the world. You are smart to take it seriously. And your child is fortunate to have <u>you</u> to take care of her.

Children and parents are special people. Enjoy this special relationship!

Notes: